PHYSICALLY
STRENGTHENED
SPIRITUALLY
DRIVEN

BY

LISA R. TYREE

PHYSICALLY STRENGTHENED

SPIRITUALLY DRIVEN

ISBN 9781733980203

Library of Congress Control Number: 2020911193

Unless otherwise indicated, all Scripture quotations are taken from King James Version unless otherwise indicated; all definition quotations are taken from web source: www.google.com. September 2018

Printed in the United States of America

First Printing, 2019
Lisa R. Tyree Publishing
Illinois

CONTENTS

ABOUT LISA RENEE TYREE

Hello, my name is Lisa Renée Tyree. I was born on October 1, 1966. I have two children who are witnesses to my incredible journey of *Physically Strengthened but Spiritually Driven*. This book is a testimony of a struggle with a life of physical difficulties and chronic pain that occurs in my life daily, even with pain medication and modern medicines that could not cure me. How my life has been with these struggles, and where God has taken me to the height of my life is, in my thinking, miraculous.

My determination to survive was made possible by the strength of God that was embedded in me. I was astonished that when I thought I would never make it, the Almighty God stepped in and carried me.

The unexpected happened to me, and my health failed at age 29 due to a workplace injury and I was placed on disability. Eventually, I was fired because I no longer could do the work. Everything began to pull me down fast. On July 11, 1996, while in my work area I suffered a severe back injury, which led to herniated discs, causing nerve damage and four back surgeries. The chronic pain affected my ability to walk, and spinal cord stimulators were placed in my back.

This book is written to help equip you and remind you it is never too late to start over again.

I was 20 years old when I had my first child, a girl, Nekeidra, and I was responsible for taking care of myself and my child. I had to find employment to support us. I was not a lazy person and was willing to work. I was a young mother and capable of achieving more in life than I had experienced previously, especially when I stayed in church and worshiped God. That was the best outcome in my life.

I started a great job with a good pay at the age of 21, working night shift. I purchased my first home at age 25, and by the age 26 I was expecting my second child, a boy whom I named Devon. No, I never married their fathers and bore my children out of wedlock. I was imperfect in my walk with God, but I knew He had forgiven me for my sins.

This book has been written to encourage someone that has chronic pain in their body along with stress and depression and does not know how to get through life challenges. From my testimony, I can tell you that it takes strength, your faith, and the belief in God to get through day to day. This has not been easy because for the past 22 years I have had to learn to live with the pain and then to begin to live my life again. I began praying harder, fasting, and praising God.

I began to get the best care, taking part in my health care and keeping appointments, going to extensive physical therapy, acupuncture, and taking medications. I also worked together with doctors using positive pain procedures at the Pain Clinic at John Stroger Hospital. I had to focus on getting better. I started expecting the blessing from God to send favor and help to manage the physical conditions in my body which I am dealing with every day.

My life started over when I received a personal relationship with Jesus Christ. My new life began in the confidence of knowing that, *I can do all things through Christ which strengthens me.* {Philippians 4:13}

To be Physically Strengthened, but Spiritually Driven is to be whole once again. My fight is to keep it moving and never to give up!

DEDICATION

I want to dedicate this book to the memory of my parents, Robert and Rutha Tyree, and a tribute to my mother whose unfailing love has defined what motherhood is all about: excellence through love. To my precious children, Nekeidra and Devon: without your love and support, I would not have made it this far to tell my story. I LOVE you dearly. My grandchildren, you keep me on my feet! Please continue to do just what you do.

Finally, to my Auntie Juanita, you have counseled me so many times and without your continued prayers, I would not be the person I am today. My dear brothers who taught me to stand and be tough and fight for what is rightful and good in my life, *My God-given Destiny*, I thank you.

ACKNOWLEDGMENTS

Thank you to design team that helped develop such a wonderful cover for my first book:
The Creative Designer (Book Cover Design)
Aaron Green
Fakulty Design LLC
Ag@fakultydesign.com

Book Photography
Ken Corbett
SKye5394@gmail.com

I want to thank Dr. Robert Watts, founder of One Flesh Ministries Bible Institute (**www.ofmbi.com**), for being a great mentor and motivational speaker, who is helping to birth new authors and helped me to accomplish my first book. I am thankful and grateful to have become a part of the IT IS WRITTEN Family of Authors.

I want to thank the best hairstylist Victoria Howard, who has worked on my hair for years and helped bring forth "Beauty out of Ashes" for me, aiding my self-confidence. She is born-again and full of wisdom. Thank you, Victoria, for keeping my hair beautiful and encouraging me.

Dr. Natalie Watts, your inspiration and talent and knowing you as my Personality Coach has been great. It has been great working with you. Pastor John Ponder, thank you for your guidance and wisdom and prayers that helped me get to my purpose in ministry. Pastor Utley, you are the man who can chase the enemies away when you lay hands on the sick, giving them strength along with recovery.

Pastor Steve Munsey, I grew in this ministry (Family Christian Center), because you are such a great Pastor, one who leads with an exceptional gift for the Kingdom of God. I thank you for the knowledge and teaching; you are my Spiritual Father in the Lord. Pastor Melodye Munsey, I thank you for being the praying woman of God who looks out for the women of Family Christian Center, and for spending the time and effort to bring to us our annual I AM Women's Conference.

FOREWORD

I am honored to write a foreword for the book, *Physically Strengthened, Spiritually Driven.* I have worked as a physician with chronic pain patients for more than 15 years and have seen some patients getting better and some dealing with pain throughout their lifetime. Ms. Tyree has been a patient of mine for a long time, and she took her healing process to another level. She describes her journey of physical and mental suffering and her faith that changed her perspective and gave her strength.

This book describes her struggles with pain, ups, downs, and how her faith helped her stay positive and motivated. The book has real-life stories that are written in an engaging and encouraging manner. Ms. Tyree wrote the book to inspire others who are dealing with struggles in their lives and helping them not to lose hope.

Dr. Taruna Waghray-Penmetch
Pain Management Specialist

Lisa came to therapy in 2016 with significant limitations in her knee motion and strength. Lisa's had determination to overcome these limitations and she worked hard, exercised, and gained significant motion, strength, and her ability to walk independently.

Thomas Zmierski DPT, OCS, CERT, MDT
The Community Hospital Fitness Pointe

Lisa R. Tyree

1

GIVING UP IS NOT AN OPTION ANYMORE

Wait on the LORD, and keep his way, and he shall exalt thee to inherit the land: when the wicked are cut off, thou shalt see it. ~Psalms 37:34

The fight to get better, to stay strong, never to give up

I was pressing my way through the pain and suffering, and I simply stood alone, waiting for something to happen at that very moment to bring relief. I was having back surgeries and health issues and taking a lot of medication and financial troubles. I even lost my employment, and it seemed I could not find my way out of the situation. I became very depressed and was unable to function at all. I called on the name of Jesus, and every step I was making He was there.

I have a great spiritual connection with my Heavenly Father who walks with me and talks with me, giving me visions and directing my path. I hate the fact that I almost gave up so many times. I knew my flesh was weak, but the more I praised God and served Him, the more I realized how much in love I was with Jesus. How can I be in love with a man I cannot see? The man I could see could not love me.

A man cannot love me the same way Jesus has loved me if each of you does not put God first. I knew without a doubt the Lord had brought me out. The Lord so many times had delivered me out of all my troubles, and every time I had an issue, He was there to pull me out of the fire. Whatever storm blew my way, God was there to protect me. I know that all these afflictions were just for the moment, but God was going to bring me joy before the battles were over. My life has had so many ups and downs.

It causes us to wonder how we can make it in this world with the loss of a job, our health, having a relationship, and your children acting up. Everyone wants to be the leader with no responsibility for their own actions. I am the person who must handle the business of saving me. "Thank you, Lord, that you have a plan for me and plans to bless me and prosper me. Lord, I know that your plans are often not the same as mine, but God, you know what the future holds for me, and I trust You."

I often remind myself that Jesus promised never to leave me or forsake me. I must trust and obey and have faith to keep going on with my life. No matter what may come or what may distract you, just know God is everywhere. Giving up may be easy to say but the outcome is often hard to accept. I believe if you give up on life, you will never know your destiny. I have not accomplished all God has for me. There are bumps in the road, but you just proceed with caution and believe you will make it. Giving up is not the same as failure; we have to focus on success. God may not come when you need him right then and there, but if He doesn't show up when we expect Him to, we must remember that His timetable is not the same as ours, and He is right on time all the time to carry us through life's difficulties.

You fail only when you give up on your destiny. You succeed when giving up is no longer an option anymore. My self-care is the best care I received: loving myself and striving for my God-given destiny. Jesus Christ is God's Son, born in a stable to Mary and her betrothed, Joseph. Jesus performed miracles and taught people about his Father God. God sent Jesus into the world to take the punishment of our sins and shame. He was the man who knew no sin, yet He died on the cross for me and for you. The God we serve raised Jesus on the third day, and Jesus now sits at the right hand of his Father God. Yes, I said it, "Giving up is not an option anymore; but living for Christ is gaining your life back until He returns and takes us to his righteous living."

1 Thessalonians 5: 9-10

"⁹ For God did not appoint us to suffer wrath but to receive salvation through our Lord Jesus Christ. ¹⁰ He died for us so that, whether we are awake or asleep, [*dead*]we may live together with him.

2

MY LIFE WITH CHRONIC PAIN

Look upon mine affliction and my pain; and forgive all my
sins. ~ Psalms 25:18

What is chronic pain and what are its effects on my life? Pain that persists for three months or longer, even after the original cause has healed, is termed chronic pain. It can evoke emotions such as fear, depression, and hopelessness, because I could not **see** the pain outside of me, but I could definitely feel the pain all over me. The feeling of isolation and despair and my emotions always out of control and feeling like a victim of my own body were the reactions that impacted my life, physically and emotionally and mentally. Taking medications and having surgery and the spinal cord stimulator in my back brought about a constant battle every day. I've lost my balance and fallen, causing me to be in worse shape with additional injuries. This made me angry, and I'd get upset and start fighting myself. I am not bitter, but I am better with the understanding that every day is not going to be a bad day. I have choices to make, and one thing I do know is the limit to my strength. I know what I can do and have gained the ability to say "no" to the things I cannot do.

Unfortunately, I had no reason to get out of bed when I was in constant pain and knowing no cure. I am not alone when it comes to family and friends offering assistance. I am not alone when it comes to Jesus, either, and He said, "Rise up and walk." When Jesus is there for you, who can be against you? I used to be so bitter about my life. Why were there so many things in my life that were going wrong at the young age of thirty? One thing I have noticed through it all is that I am not bitter; but I am better at dealing with the pain and limitations because of my faith, and my family and church family prayed. We wonder why bad things happen to good people... stop the press, if nothing is going wrong in your life, you cannot experience the mercy and grace of calling on Jesus in both the bad times and the good times. I called on him all the time.

My God is not a fan of "ugly," and not pleased with "pretty," either. Let me make it clear, if you treat people unkindly, rudely, uncaringly, and with selfishness, you will look like one with bad pride. How can the Lord work with you on healing you of cancer and heart disease and your physical condition? There is no place in God's kingdom for arrogance! The level of your attitude will control the level of your circumstances as well as the level of your success in life. I know this is true. If I let my good days outweigh my bad days, I will never have a better day. The Lord wants my best work, not my complaint.

I am so inspired by my pastor and his strength to continue in faith, teaching the people about deliverance, salvation, and healing. It is all about loving yourself and forgiving others who hurt you. That is when you need to pray more. My lessons on living with chronic back pain have taught me that everything I experience in life has some sort of lesson that I am going to learn. If I will face it with an overwhelming degree of letting it go, I will feel better in all aspects of my life.

What chronic pain does is to transform you from an overcoming person to a pitiful patient. It is a lesson I dealt with for twenty-three years of fighting with pain, being constantly afraid of never getting better. In that condition, it was difficult to focus on anything else but pain.

People say that everything we experience in life has some sort of lesson that we are going to learn. When you are faced with something so overwhelming that you let every good thing in your life go, it was difficult to "get" the lesson I should have. I couldn't think straight or get a good night's rest because of pain. It was impossible to believe that there was any type of lesson at all to learn.

In the last twenty-three years of fighting with chronic pain and fearful of what tomorrow was going to bring or otherwise right at this moment. I had a difficult time staying focused due to the pain. My focus was on when I

could take the next dose of pain medication all the time. I believed that if only I could get rid of the pain, my life would be manageable once again.

My problem was that on days when I experienced less pain, I was so fearful of pain returning that I stood still and did nothing. This made my condition worse and it became a growing problem. I had to keep moving, you see. Because I was too focused on getting relief, eventually I realized that it wasn't the pain that was controlling my life—it was fear. I was afraid and had all kinds of treatment for pain and all kinds of medications.

I had four back surgeries with a spinal cord stimulation in my spine for eight years to help with damaged nerves in my back. Amazingly, I began going to church and believing for my healing and for deliverance from this crippling pain. I realized my fear was the controlling factor in my life. I was able to think it over and claim my life back. I am in control, not my pain.

I had to stop pushing the panic button and believe that God is with me. There's no need to fear, for my God is with me. He will hold me steady and keep a firm hand on me. I prayed this prayer, "Lord I place my life and body in your hands today. Please, Lord, guide the medical professionals who will work on this body. Give them skills and wisdom and guide their hands and minds. Use them to restore me to health that you may be glorified." I had four surgeries on my spine from January 1997 to August 2013 when they removed the spinal cord stimulator. My family and friends had prayed for me before I went to surgery, and yes, I was very nervous each time.

I prayed for the doctors and nurses that were going to take care of me. My best friend Jesus Christ was present every time, spiritually speaking. I was fearful I was going to be cut on again and I questioned Him. What if something goes wrong? What if there are complications? Will I ever feel like myself again? How much pain will I have to face during the recovery process? I prayed, "In the midst of all the fears, Lord, I will cling to You. I am terrified, but nevertheless, I will put my trust in You."

Psalm 29:11

The Lord gives strength to

his people:

The Lord blesses his people

with peace.

3

1 AM AN OVERCOMER AND TAKING CONTROL

The Lord is Faithful, and he will Strengthen and protect you. – 2 Thessalonians 3:3

I needed to put happiness and joy back into my life. I was responsible for my body and my life. I was 29 years old when I injured my back at work on July 11, 1996. I had worked twelve hours that day, I will never forget that day. That is the day when I felt my life ended. I was working, and in lifting a heavy pan of chocolate that night I felt a snap in my back and sharp pain. I was sent to the emergency room by my manager. I was in so much pain — and I was alone. After treatment and tests, I was sent back to work that night in a cab; then I had to get in my car and drive home in a lot of pain. I was called to work the next morning by the company nurse. I complied and returned to work, but I still was in a lot of pain because I could not take the medicine the emergency room gave me.

I had to suffer for four more hours before the nurse at the company sent me to their company doctor's office. They did not have my best interests when it came to my health. I was given some stronger medicine and, of course, sent back to work. This was no problem since I liked what I was doing at my workplace. I was a Senior Operator Shift Leader.

At the same time, I was a full-time mom taking care of my two children. I continued to work, and I was not getting better, experiencing excruciating pain in my lower back and my right leg.

The pain continued to get worse, and I kept working long hours at the job until one day I couldn't move anymore. I had cared more about working than I cared that my own body was breaking down. The pain was out of control, and I could not function at all. The company, of course, knew my physical condition, but I did not get the memo or the results of my tests that showed a herniated disk problem that had the nerves trapped. This was so unexpectedly difficult to go through alone. I was having problems walking and I fell at work. I was taken off work and was started on treatment with an epidural block in my back. After the third epidural within three weeks, I was sent back to work. I complied and went back to work and brought with me 20lbs of weight due to steroids. This put more pressure on my back and legs. I was placed on light duty. Working eight hours instead of twelve hours now; nevertheless, the pain grew worse again the second day at work.

I could not take the medications at work, because it had the tendency to make me drowsy and unable to function properly at work. It was hard to manage the pain in my lower back and right leg. This was the stage called acute pain, the sensation you feel when there is damage or danger to your body. For example, as doctors explained to me, it is like placing your hand against a hot surface which causes acute pain. The amount of acute pain you will experience at the first onset of pain. This will alert you that you have damage somewhere in your body and is causing you severe pain.

I had to adjust and live a day at a time. That kept me going even through my darkest days. I learned that my pain experience did affect my quality of life and my family. I had to take control and decide about having surgery on my back to relieve the nerves that were trapped. This pain was never going to get better, and I became very emotional. I felt hopeless and helpless and guilty. I could not believe that this had happened to me.

I had to go through sleepless nights trying to overcome the pain in my physical body. The limitations imposed by my physical condition and the pressure in my spine were unbearable. I had been dealing with the pain for six months before I decided to go for the first back surgery in 1997. I made the choice so I could get back to a normal life again.

After having the surgery, I thought that I would bounce back to the person I was before the injuries and their accompanying pain affected my life. I was wrong. The pain came back after three to four weeks of trying to heal. One day I was in my bathroom and was combing my hair, and I felt a powerful muscle spasm up my back. I passed out on the floor in front of my children. My daughter called the emergency number and ran and got my neighbor. When I awoke, they were crying. My daughter was ten years old and my son was three years old; this was frightening for my children. I was rushed to the hospital. I became involved in learning about chronic pain. This came in the form of a self-help program to gain a better understanding of my pain and how I can regain control of my life. This was reason enough to be proud of taking control of my life. The plan is to have faith. *Even so faith, if it hath not works, it is dead.* James 2:20

I had to be instrumental in my own health because we must keep God's temple free from being overtaken by Satan's attacks. I learned my body is not my own, but it is God's property. It was God that kept me because I almost gave up. The depression had me down, and I had terrible thoughts, but God's mercy is what brought me through. I needed a spiritual uplift to keep my physical body and my emotions under control until my change came.

James 2:20

But wilt thou know, O vain man, that

faith without works is dead?

4

I AM LIVING AND I SHALL NOT DIE

I shall not die, but live, and declare the works of the LORD.
-Psalms 118:17

Chronic back and leg pain have changed my life. It has brought about real trials and tribulations; many days I felt like giving up. My children were very young, and my family members had to go on this journey with me. My physical conditions were worsened by anxiety, fear, and depression, and I was placed on disability. I learned that having chronic back and leg pain that arose from the herniated disk and sciatica nerve damage was not going away any time soon.

I had to get a better understanding of what I was dealing with on top of moving around with the support of mobility devices. My first back surgery in 1997 was a difficult surgery. I was told that the nerves in my back were damaged and would take a while to heal, but I was admonished, "Do not give up." How can I give up when I am only thirty years old with small children? The extensive physical therapy began to help me walk and accept that I am not going to be crippled for the rest of my life. I pushed myself aggressively trying to make something happen in the short term so I could get back to work.

I experienced the most important thing on this journey. Being young does not guarantee you will get better fast and pushing yourself beyond your limits is a bad idea. I was dedicated to getting the job done to return to normal. My thinking did not consult with my body that was broken down, leaving difficulties that will take time to heal. The pain in my lower back was a distressingly permanent and highly uncomfortable feeling. I was going to physical therapy three times a week, and family members had adjusted their schedules to help me with my children and transportation.

I could not drive at this time and my car was a two-door small sports car 1996, Mitsubishi 3000 GT that was fast and very low. I could not get into this vehicle after spinal surgery. I had to depend on others to drive me around in their vehicles. I was not happy at all, and the push to get better only prevented me from recovering from the surgery. I started feeling hopeless and helpless, a poor mother to my children. I felt life just stop and my back condition never improved because I couldn't do anything at this point. I had made plans to marry in 1997 to Mr. Thurman, the father of my son, and I had planned the wedding at the beginning of 1996. We both worked for the same employer and had the same twelve-hours work schedule.

The wedding did not happen because of the back injuries sustained on the job that left me unable to walk or go to the destination wedding planned. I could not get around at all. This is when I became very depressed and

just wanted to give up. I was more focused on my life going down and disappointment about my health. I had to call the wedding off. At this point I needed God's help and deliverance for I was feeling powerless.

I was missing something in my life, and I felt so guilty and empty and discouraged that I could not believe that my life was over at thirty years old. I started watching TD Jakes Ministries on the gospel station, and I had already read the book, *Woman Thou Art Loosed.* I was missing a connection with the Lord. Somehow, an amazing thing happened: I started praying. The man of God, TD Jakes, said I shall live, and I shall not die. This inspired me to search the Bible scripture until I found it and hope came alive in me. I received a call from Mother Jackson, an Apostolic Holy Ghost woman from Refuge Temple Church, who invited my children and me to an Apostolic Pentecostal Convention in Milwaukee for the weekend. My mother, Ruth, volunteered to drive us to Milwaukee. My children and I packed up, and we went to the Holy Convocation on November 7, 1997.

I was happy to be in the presence of the Lord, and I was looking to be physically healed. The amazing thing did happen; I was just sitting in my chair and listening to the Pastors of the Church of Our Lord Jesus Christ of the Apostolic Faith, and they begin speaking in Spiritual Tongues over me and I was caught up in the Spirit. The Church was filled with believers praising God. I was feeling something in my body shifting. My mother and

children, who were concerned about my physical conditions, were fearful something bad was happening.

I went down on the floor and a transformation took place. I started speaking in another language that I never knew existed. My relationship with the Lord Jesus Christ began to emerge in me like living water cleansing my body. The next week I was invited to the Refuge Temple Church for their baptismal service and asked if I were ready to go down in Jesus' name for the remission of sin. I was filled with the Holy Ghost speaking in tongues as the Bible states in {Act 2:38- 42}.

38 Then Peter said unto them, Repent, and be baptized every one of you in the name of Jesus Christ for the remission of sins, and ye shall receive the gift of the Holy Ghost.

39 For the promise is unto you, and to your children, and to all that are afar off, even as many as the Lord our God shall call.

40 And with many other words did he testify and exhort, saying, Save yourselves from this untoward generation.

41 Then they that gladly received his word were baptized: and the same day there were added unto them about three thousand souls.

42 And they continued steadfastly in the apostles' doctrine and fellowship, and in breaking of bread, and in prayers.

I begin living again and learning about the Son, Jesus Christ, and what He sacrificed for my sins on the cross. I knew about God but not the story of Jesus Christ the Lord and Savior. I was instantly focused on beating the chronic pain and the depression. I had hope and a renewed relationship with my children and family; I vowed not to walk in the flesh but after the Spirit.

I was in attendance for Sunday School every Sunday morning faithfully. Now I had a purpose to learn about Jesus and the miracles He performed while here on earth. I learned about the healing of the blind and His causing the lame to walk and His healing all diseases, the woman with the issue of blood—and even me. I was still on assisted mobility devices to walk but I was not giving up.

Many other people whom I knew and/or heard about wanted to give up and die due to their health issues. I could not function normally in my physical body; I was functioning in my spiritual new body. The Lord had chosen me for such a time as this to test my faith. I began to feel like a female Job in the Bible who lost everything, including his health, and children, and servants, and livestock; and even his wife, who wanted him to curse God and die.

Why did I choose this as a chapter in my book? In this world, you have a choice to live for Christ or die to sin and shame. I wanted to live righteously, but I was still a baby in Christ. I lost my health and relationships and

employment, but I gained Christ. It is never too late, and Jesus is never too busy to help you out of your situations no matter what the issues of life bring. He is there for you forever. The hard work began, and I was promoted to Sunday School teacher, working with the youth department. I started studying missionary lessons in the ministries and speaking at my church for our missionary service. I was promoted to the next level: a Social Missionary with license credential of the Apostolic Faith Headquarters of New York, New York under Apostle Bishop Bonner on August 14, 2001.

The enemy setback was only a setup for a comeback to serve the Lord Jesus Christ. I began to fight the good fight of faith. My new employer now was working and building the Kingdom of God. I found my purpose for living and loving my life.

Isaiah 54:17

No weapon that is formed against thee shall prosper; and every tongue that shall rise against thee in judgment thou shalt condemn. This is the heritage of the servants of the LORD, and their righteousness is of me, saith the LORD.

5

1 HAVE TO BEAT SATAN RUNNING

"Let us run with perseverance the race marked out for us."
~ Hebrews 12:1

Why did I come up with this topic? Well, it is simply saying what is on my mind: I am tired of Satan running behind me and around me playing his game. I feel it is time to run behind Satan and give him a chase in Jesus' name!

James 1:12-14 blessed is the man that endured temptation for when he is tried, he shall receive the crown of life, which the Lord hath promised to them that love him.

I was frustrated and ashamed of my physical conditions, tired of dealing with limitations caused by my chronic pain. I was in control of neither my body functions nor my life. It was a living hell that I needed to depend on others for help with my children and making sure my bills were paid on time. I know the devil's work is to steal and kill and destroy my destiny. I was powerless to fight on my own and I had to beat the devil running for my life.

Life without Jesus Christ is like having an empty soul, which makes us so hungry for spiritual food, the Word of God. I must stay full on Jesus Christ's love for me and reading the Word of God to beat Satan in his game.

He is always testing the faith of the child of God, trying to make him or her give up on the Lord. The enemy is a snake such as in the Garden of Eden. The first woman, Eve, was tempted so she could receive knowledge and power, and she wanted Adam to disobey God. Because of disobedience, the curse of birthing pain was introduced to Eve's life and has been extended down generational lines to every woman after her to endure the same pain.

The Lord God said unto the serpent, *Because thou hast done this, thou art cursed above all cattle, and above every beast of the field: upon thy belly shalt thou go, and dust shalt thou eat all the days of thy life.* I saw that the enemy wanted to bring bad and deceptive news to our ears. I learned to deal with him by talking in spiritual tongues and getting into my Bible, finding scriptures that are so powerful informing us that when we call on the name of Jesus, that evil spirit will flee.

The LORD shall cause thine enemies that rise up against thee to be smitten before thy face: they shall come out against thee one way and flee before thee seven ways. ~Deuteronomy 28:7

I made the right decision to serve God with all my heart and soul because I love Him. I was going through my physical pain and now there were other conditions diagnosed. I have osteoarthritis joint disease in my knees and in my spine now. I was upset to learn this news from the doctors. I was also told by my employer to go on short-term disability, but I was hurt on the job. Eventually, in

1999, I was let go because the spinal surgery in 1997 was not successful due to previously injured nerves that damaged my spine. Afterward, I could not do that line of work anymore. I was not considered a team player to my employer anymore. I felt all my accomplishments were lost. I went from making $60,000 in 1996 to making $29,208.00. I lost half my income being off work and, of course, there were more medical bills unpaid. I was trying to return to work so I would not lose my employment, but there was no light duty work per management.

I felt like one of God's faithful characters in the Bible, a female Job. The story is that Job was a good man who honored God. Job was healthy and very rich. The devil dared God and took everything away from Job because he thought that Job would not obey God if Job was poor and sick. God let the devil have his way with Job, but Satan couldn't take his life. The bad things began to happen to Job and he lost animals and servants; all his children were killed by fire. Job himself, became very ill, but he still did not deny God because his faithfulness and righteousness were inbred in him. The Lord blessed him double for all his trouble and Job was healed. When I was down and out of work and was going through my savings and my children's college money that I had saved, I remembered Job's fight to win against the devil. The story of Job encouraged me to be determined that I will stand and wait on the Lord for my double blessing.

I started running my race without fear and trembling. I decided it is never too late to choose to be saved in Jesus' name, and to be held in the palm of his hands, where no one can take you out.

My life had not been easy walking with a walker, but I am a fighter, and I was not turning my back on the Lord when it comes to a battle between Jesus and Satan. I was assured if I walk with Jesus and look to Him, I can beat Satan running because Jesus Christ now had my life. I know Jesus has never failed me yet.

The Lord God is interested in the tests and trials that I will win by continuing praising Him. My faith in God is the reason I can give a testimony that my race is not yet finished, but a double blessing is on the way if I will never give up.

There are many enemies who don't want you to die to this old-world system; they want you in their control. But to live for Christ brings you a better life. I am here to tell you and proclaim that although the devil may send his armies to defeat me. I have no enemies and they do not have me.

Submit yourselves therefore to God. Resist the devil, and he will flee from you. ~ James 4:7

I do not complain about my circumstances around me anymore. I do not want to be a double-minded woman that is unstable in all my ways. I am not allowing Satan to continue to attack my mind and body. I am so happy that The Lord promised of the gift of the Holy Ghost to teach and train you for battle against the Prince of this world. I received the gift for discerning of spirits after I was filled with the Holy Ghost. I thank the Lord Jesus Christ for protecting me from the hands of the enemy.

The enemy of God has so many names and workers on this earth, and if Satan had known who he was destroying, he would never have done the horrible action that caused Jesus' crucifixion. Have you ever been disappointed by people who say they have your back, but they are really trying to destroy your life? I just call on the name of Jesus and He will come quickly to defend me. I have had to be strong and courageous against whatever situation I was against, turning that problem around. When the person or problem becomes a burden, I just keep calling on the name of Jesus. Trust me: He will send His angels to fight on your behalf and bring down the high places that you fear. We must know who we are and whose we are. We are representatives of the Lord of Hosts. He will fight for you if you never quit.

Mark 16: 15-18

And He said go ye in to all the world and preach the gospel to every creature. He that believes and is baptized shall be saved: but he that believes not shall be damned, and these signs shall follow them that believe, in Jesus name they shall cast out devils: they shall speak with new tongues. They shall take up serpents: and if they drink any deadly thing, it shall not hurt them, they shall lay hands on the sick, and they shall recover.

6

I MUST PROCEED WITH CAUTION AT ALL TIMES

Be strong and of good courage; for the Lord your God. He is the one who goes with you. He will not leave you nor forsake you. ~ Joshua 1:9

What has living with pain taught me? My chronic pain came in a variety of ways and degrees of intensity. My pain is associated with multiple physical problems in my body. The pain medications don't always work to relieve all my pain. My pain has taught me that patience and compliance with doctor's orders can win respect and confidence that the medications that I needed to have a smidgen of relief on my road to recovery will be available to me. The doctors referred me to a pain management specialist to manage the pain with other options.

I had to be taught about my vertebra and the nervous system. I needed to know why I am not recovering quickly as I want to be healed. The nervous system controls and coordinates all organs and the structure of the human body. The misalignment of the spinal vertebrae and discs may cause irritation to the nervous system, which could affect the structures, organs, and functionality. I have now been shown pictures from my MRI, and have a better understanding about why I am
having difficulties with my lower back and lower limbs and walking.

I must proceed with caution so I can recover and get back to a normal life again. My discs and the nerves in my back were damaged on the premises of my employer. I did not know the importance of my body structure as a woman and the things we should not do with our bodies (example: lifting heavy objects that will snap your back and cause trauma to the nerve). The lumbar spine contains several discs and nerves that cause a very serious situation when the nerves are trapped by herniation. When you go so long without treatment and knowledge, you are prevented from getting better. The medications only cover the pain; they do not heal the condition. Seek medical attention and please learn what is precisely wrong with your body. Keep asking until you understand, and make sure you get details.

The injuries I sustained affected my lower lumbar L4-L5, L5-S1. This was very serious, and it painfully affected my lower back a well as my bladder and knees. The sciatic nerve and lower legs, which led to poor circulation in the legs, and weakness and muscle cramps were also affected. It has affected the buttocks with sacroiliac conditions and spinal curvatures. I had limitations in sitting and walking and standing for even short periods of time.

I could not do any physical activities. I was referred for a work functional capacity assessment by my employer's doctor. I was not able to walk on the treadmill and had fallen. I was referred to physical therapy to help strengthen my spine and legs. I was complying so I could get better in order to return to work.

I pushed myself to the point that I began to cry often because I was in excruciating pain and discomfort. I did not want to see anyone, and my children were afraid, because my pain had led me to end my relationship with their father. I was afraid that I was not going to survive. I was stressed and not sleeping very well, and just felt helpless. I prayed for help and I was given strong pain medication such as opioids and anti-inflammatory medicine.

I cannot tolerate some medication, that had me in the bed with side effects. I was having many bad days, experiencing panic attacks and anxiety. One day while on an elevator in downtown Chicago, I had a muscle spasm in my back that knocked me off my feet and I passed out. I woke up in the ambulance on the way to the hospital with my mother beside me praying. I did not know what had happened to me. The emergency room doctor put me on bed restriction and fall prevention.

I went back to my pain management team of doctors who referred me to a pain psychologist, because I was not accepting my physical condition all that well. I went from a temporary disability to a permanent disability. I was not happy being labeled "disabled" at the young age of 35, but

that was the facts. I was struggling to accept the science of the mind, its nature and functions in dealing with PTSD.

Trust in the Lord with all your heart and lean not on your own understanding: In all your ways acknowledge Him. And He shall direct your paths. ~Proverbs 3:5-6

I was dealing with depression and had no knowledge of what that was like. I had never dealt with depression in my life. I was happy before the injury in 1996 and now it is 2001, and I am depressed. The pain psychologist helped me to accept the pain, to learn all I can about my physical condition, to understand that there may be no current cure. I needed to deal with the fact that pain in my life is permanent.

I had to take an active role in my own recovery. I had to follow instructions from my doctors to move from a passive role into one in partnership in my health care. I had to do water exercise because unused muscles feel more pain and no exercise leaves you weak. I had to start slowly, safely building up strength in my body.

The word <u>physic</u> in the dictionary is the art of healing disease: practice of medicine, an internal medicine. The word <u>strength</u> is quality or state of being strong: ability to do or to bear with force and power. I craved that power to resist attacks and intensity of pain. The word <u>spiritual</u> is pertaining to the spirit and the soul or pertaining to sacred things of the Church.

My children were very worried about me; my parents, as well as others, expressed great concern. I was not functioning or handling my disability well at all. I needed help to get better and believe in my strength. I was willing to make changes to take good care of myself and my children. I moved from my house for a while to live with my parents to help with my children and help myself. I did not give up; I was willing to fight for my right to be healed.

Psalm 27:1

The Lord is my light and my salvation:
whom shall, I fear? The Lord is the strength
of my life; of whom shall I be afraid?

7

I HAVE NO TIME TO COMPLAIN

Now faith is the substance of things hoped for, the evidence of things not seen. ~Hebrews 11:1

I took the next step by playing an active role in my recovery for pain control. I went back to the pain management team and started the rehabilitation to get restored to useful life through education and therapy. I stopped looking for pain relief and started living my life with the pain. The reason I didn't complain is I wanted to be physically and spiritually well. My mind-set was "I am going to be successful in accomplishing my goals."

The best plan was to move back with my parents and get help with my children. My daughter was fifteen and my son was nine and given my physical limitations, I was not capable of giving them the best care alone. This put a huge burden and stress on my relationship with those siblings for years.

The great thing that helped get myself together was my mother. She was bold and a woman of God. The help I received from my family was the road to recovery and it was not easy. I had to have faith and trust Jesus for my healing. I had no time to stop; it was time to get with the program.

I was in denial for such a long time and praying to my Lord and Savior Jesus Christ for help. I needed to get back to a normal life. I went from independent living to depending on my parents for help. I needed to take control and have some stability for my children; they were suffering with me. I looked back at my past achievement to start focusing on the present. I had no time for misery as company any longer.

The combination of painkiller medications and my physical impairment had caused other conditions in my body. I was dealing with obesity. The fact was that I had gained weight over the years due to taking steroid medications and injections often to relieve pain and inflammation in my spine and knees. This was a continuing routine year after year.

I visited my primary physician and I avoided complaining about pain because I did not want more or stronger pain medicines added to my list of medications. I wanted adequate pain relief, but the side effects and my functional impairment had only brought on other conditions.

The negative result of taking medication is impairment in functioning or a decrease in quality of life and a restricted lifestyle. I continued to focus on pain, and I was very defensive and feeling misunderstood. I am not against medication or the physician that prescribes medication to help me. I am against the side effects that hurt me and having to take another medication to help primary medications. Example: constipation and allergic reactions and hives. I am simply making a statement of facts that I read in the instructions on my prescription pamphlets as well as personal experience with the medications prescribed to me.

The Health Psychology referred me to a Chronic Pain Support Group in the hospital. This was my first instance of seeing many people having the same health issues in the same room together. I saw people struggling with their disabilities, and others who apparently didn't have a disability. They all had some type of life crisis that happened to them producing their need to come for support. There were older people and young people in this group. I felt confident that I was in the right place for a breakthrough.

I was not going to share my story with the group and break down in tears after two weeks of coming. They asked if I wanted to share anything about my history of chronic pain and my experience. I could only reply, "When is it going to stop hurting and when am I going to get better? This physical condition is horrible, and I can't tolerate it anymore." I had no one else I could complain to because they couldn't understand. I was suffering greatly all the time and did not recognize there are all kinds of pain. Some chronic pains come from diseases that are curable, and some are not curable and will lead to death.

I realized my pain was not near death. I needed to grow stronger in my belief that I will regain control of my body. I reached out to my health care providers and started setting priorities to get involved with treatment. I wanted to have a plan for exploring any other ways to control the pain. I had to be assertive. I had a right to have my pain treated appropriately. My pain is controllable, and I am not allowing my pain to control me.

The treatments may fail, but God's promises will stand and be fulfilled in every person who is dealing with chronic disease or pain.

My prayer: "Lord, help me to help others understand that you control everything, and your will is 'yes' and 'amen' to heal us and deliver us, to restore your people from all hurt and pain and misery. I will always trust you, Lord, and thank you for my pain, because it led me to you, I will always serve you."

Colossians 1:11

Strengthened with all might, according to his glorious power, unto all patience and longsuffering with joyfulness;

8

CAN THESE DRY BONES LIVE AGAIN?

And he said unto me, Son of man, can these bones live? And I answered, O Lord GOD, thou knowest. Ezekiel 37:3

The Lord told Ezekiel to prophesy upon the bones he saw, and he did what was commanded of him. He prophesied and there was a noise, and behold a shaking and bones came together bone to bone.

The Old Testament prophet Ezekiel is one of the four great prophets in the Bible. He had suffered a great loss. Ezekiel was taken captive for eleven years before the destruction of Jerusalem, and his wife died of a stroke. The prophet Ezekiel continued in the Lord's works until his death.

I am a witness to my own dry bones, and there is a story to be told. In the previous chapters, you learned about my history of pain and suffering. I am going to explain all that I experienced and learned. I will not give up the fight! With the Lord on my side I will be a conqueror.

My lower back pain and leg pain was frustrating to me and to my physicians. The pain was severe in that I always felt the pain traveling from lower back, radiating down to my knees and legs and toes. I was having muscle spasms after lifting anything. It was putting a strain on my back. I was sent to the hospital for x-rays followed up with a Magnetic Resonance Imaging (MRI) test to confirm the diagnosis. There was a herniated disc in the two-level that was pinching the nerves causing the sciatic pain.

I had the first surgery in 1997: a laminectomy and discectomy to remove a partially herniated disc. My second back surgery in 2005 was for a spinal cord stimulator implant. The spinal cord stimulator that sent an electrical charge failed. I had a third back surgery in 2006 for revision of a new and improved neurological spinal cord stimulator to be implanted. I could now charge the battery pack from home with the new technology of computers. This was the new and improved system that was conquering the pain. I was very happy with the system—it worked for me. The spinal cord stimulator's purpose was to control the pain and fire up the nerves. I did come back to life again with this new program. I again started physical therapy; I was able to move back home with my children. I went back to Triton College in River Grove for Health Information Administration.

I was having pain episodes in school from walking along with sitting too long in class, although I had a walker and a cane. I was having joint pain in my knees which caused me to be unstable I wobbled a lot walking. I could not completely straighten or bend my knees without sharp pain and stiffness. My knees were so weak getting up and ready for school that I missed class and went to the hospital emergency department. I had an x-ray of my knees, another examination, and was given medication for inflammation. I learned a new diagnosis—again, disappointing news. I went to my primary physician with my results in addition to a new referral to a clinic for my knee problems.

I have osteoarthritis, a chronic degeneration of the cartilage of the joints, with fibromyalgia on top of that. These conditions were the source of the problems with my bones and muscles. My knees were strong once upon a time. Now with the weight gain and stress on the joint, I could not tolerate standing on them for very long. I was limited now on continuing to finish what I started in my education. I finished my course but never took the broad test.

I avoided activities that made the pain worse and began gentle exercise and pool therapy. My therapist recommended acupuncture and acupressure to help relax the muscle and pain. This pain was affecting my sleeping at night. I went to Chicago Chinatown for Chinese medicine and the price was not cheap. I paid out of my pocket to get the treatment.

I explained this treatment to my physicians, and they referred me to Cook County Hospital where the treatment for acupuncture costs less. The practitioner's name was Dr. Wicks, an African American professional that knew I explained this treatment to my physicians, and they referred me to Cook County Hospital where the treatment for acupuncture costs less. The practitioner's name was Dr. Wicks, an African American professional that knew the ancient Chinese practice, the use of ultra-thin needles placed in my body for back and knee pain. These little needles stimulate the anatomical points and help to reduce stress and ease pain (ex. arthritis and fibromyalgia). The disposable needles are under clean and sterile conditions by a qualified practitioner. The complications are very minimal. The highly trained practitioner knows what they are doing and was highly recommended to ease the pain for my healing.

I was on so many medications and treatments for so long that other illnesses started forming against my body. In 2007 I was diagnosed with type-2 diabetes and hypertension along with hyperlipidemia. This was stressful to deal with and the depression and anxiety attacks increased. I had spent all my money on prescription drugs and many physicians only to keep going back and finding out new physical problems. I was doomed to deal with every day of my life.

I was forty years old at this time, but my body felt like I was seventy years old. I had been seeing the rheumatologist for a year receiving treatments of knee injections and steroids in addition to pain medication. I was referred out to see an orthopedic surgeon for my bilateral knee pain which had caused weakness and difficulties with walking. I was already walking with a walker, and, as a result of less exercise and steroids, I had gained so much weight. I had to stop and sit or stand still until the pain subsided, then begin to walk again until I got to my destination.

The rheumatology doctor referred me to an orthopedic clinic and the examination revealed significant crepitant sounds bilaterally and my range of motion was at a low degree. The plan and recommendations were a total knee arthroplasty. My condition was significantly advanced. I had to think about a total knee replacement and return to the clinic in six weeks. My life again took on another disappointment and difficult decision to make. I returned to the orthopedic clinic and declined to have the surgery at that time. I needed to wait on the Lord Jesus Christ for restoration and healing naturally. I signed up for another mobility aid: a Jazzy scooter from the scooter store to ride around and keep the pressure off my knees.

I rode the scooter for several months and I was not active. My top weight was two-hundred and eighty pounds, and if I had continued to truck around in that scooter, I would not have fought to get better. I joined a fitness center for aqua classes that teach arthritis movement in the warm water. I was determined to get these bones moving. The Lord's question to the prophet Ezekiel, "Can these bones live again?" My answer is yes, my Lord, they will live again in this year of 2009. I already had in my body a spinal cord stimulator. This physically helps with the transmission of natural electricity in the body. The Lord breathes life in Him, the hope of glory, into my Spiritual body. The spoken word is " Never ever give up; always keep the faith."

The Lord is a healer and He will deliver me from all my affliction and condition. I will stand on the promises of God my Savior.

Psalms 103:1-5

1 Bless the LORD, O my soul: and all that is within me, bless his holy name.

2 Bless the LORD, O my soul, and forget not all his benefits:

3 Who forgiveth all thine iniquities; who healeth all thy diseases;

4 Who redeemeth thy life from destruction; who crowneth thee with lovingkindness and tender mercies;

5 Who satisfieth thy mouth with good [things; so that] thy youth is renewed like the eagle's.

9

DO NOT GIVE UP THE FIGHT

God is our refuge and strength, a very present help in trouble. ~Psalm 46:1

I often wondered how all these conditions, pain and suffering, came upon me. I asked the question to the Lord, "Why me?" My life without Jesus Christ will be the end. There is no end when Jesus is in your life. I must go through my tests and trials, tribulations to face what will come in my future. I know who I am in Christ, and I will surrender and trust in the Lord. I will endure while rejoicing in His grace until my situation can be reversed, while I wait on the Lord to restore me.

I went on a spiritual prayer and fasting program, putting my flesh on notice that I expected it to obey, and, through faith, I would be strengthened. The pain had always been a part of my life, but each day I reminded myself that despite the pain I still had the ability to live. I chose to be transformed and have no fear that pain may restrict me or prevent me from making plans to live my life. My focus should not be driven by pain. I was determined to focus on praying to God to heal my physical conditions and to increase my faith that with His help I would be supported to spiritually fight for restoration and deliverance.

The hidden disability that people could not see in me was the spinal cord stimulator in my back that was sending low electric pulses directly into my spinal cord to relieve pain. The spinal cord stimulator is used most often after non-surgical pain treatment options have failed to provide sufficient relief. I had to be very careful about going through metal detectors in stores and airport scanners. I had to keep an identification card stating I have a machine in me and/or try to bypass these areas so it would not cause me harm.

There is always a surprise in life that will test your patience and your faith. I had already been tried and tested enough. I learned that life's difficulties are there to make you strong. The fight is tough, and the battle does not belong to me; but when God is for me who can be against me? There shalt not be any fear come over me for what this world has to offer me. The words of the Lord tell us no good things will He withhold from you if you walk uprightly before Him. (*See Psalms 84:11.*) I know change will come and that faith works together with patience. I cannot give up the fight no matter if I fall down several times. I will get back up again and move forward, knowing God's goodness and mercy shall follow me all the days of my life.

I visited a church in Chicago called Bethlehem Healing Temple. I was amazed when I walked in on my walker. They greeted me and asked me if this were my first time at their church. I replied, "No my cousin who is a Bishop named David preached here last week." I felt the presence of the anointing over me bringing about a desire for a return visit to get another dose of spiritual healing for my soul. They all started praying in tongues: it was not my physical condition that they looked on but my eagerness to bypass the "problem me," and focus on the spiritual side of "me." Along with two prayer warriors, I was directed to the prayer room where these women prayed over me strongly before I joined the members in the sanctuary. I was at the right place at the right time for the fight of my life.

I began going to the church Bible studies on Tuesdays and attending church on Sundays, becoming involved with their Missionary Department. The church had a nursing home ministry. We went out two by two to teach about Jesus and His saving grace. I was around strong saints of God who bound up spirits and people were healed, and deliverance came to these individuals in the nursing home.

I began leading and speaking at nursing home. My team would bring in refreshments and clothing to the residents. The smiles and the respect from the workers also made it clear we were welcome.

I continued my journey there until my mother was diagnosed in 2009 with ovarian cancer stage four. This was another strike from the devil against my family. I started praying in the prayer room more often at church. I began to take my mother there so she could feel the presence of the Holy Spirit. My mother was in church faithfully throughout her lifetime and was baptized and served as a staff nurse at her church. She never had been baptized in Jesus' name. I tried my best to get my mother to be re-baptized in Jesus' name and be filled with the Holy Ghost as stated in Acts 2:38-39. I thank God my mother is saved by serving and her faith in God.

I stopped attending Bethlehem Healing Church in 2009 and for support, stayed with my mother in south suburban Lansing. The battles of the cancer and seeing her in and out of the hospital for surgery were strong. The chemotherapy was hard on my mother and the health insurance was giving her a hard time paying for the chemotherapeutic treatment. My mother never gave up or let me feel sorry for what she was going through, however. My depression returned full force, and I needed to seek counseling right away.

My cousin, Ray Vanhook, is a member of Family Christian Center Church in Munster Indiana. I went to a **Sunday morning** church service with my cousin to praise and worship to help me calm down. Pastor Steve Munsey was teaching and demonstrating from the Bible. I enjoyed the service and the illustrations of the Word of God.

I enjoyed the service and went up to the visitor reception and was welcomed. I started attending the church as a guest while staying with my mother and encouraging her to stay strong.

I came back to church for a **Friday morning** prayer and met Pastors Steve and Melodye Munsey and asked for prayer for my mother. They gave me great information and inspiration on dealing with cancer. Unfortunately, I didn't succeed in getting my mother baptized in Jesus' name before she passed on New Year's Day in 2011. I was there when she made her transition and I anointed her body with oil, and I know she is with the Lord in heavenly places. My mother paid her tithes until her death, and she taught me to be strong and courageous and never giving up the fight, staying strong. My mother was my hero and my rock and was strong in the faith.

My loved ones grieved heavily for the loss of my Mother Ruth. She gave birth to six children. The firstborn was a girl who spent six months of life on earth and is in heaven. There are the three brothers that are older than I, and finally, my mother got her girl—me—and later a little brother. I was the only girl with four brothers. Life was rough growing up with a house full of boys and an adopted uncle. My mother took care of everybody's children in the neighborhood and they called her Mama T.

When I say I was tough and rough as a young girl with all males in the house, I mean it. It was a battlefield for real. My next book, due to release in 2020, will have more details.

Recovery after the loss of my mother was difficult and overwhelming. I had to start all over again. I began to take charge of all aspects of my life both physically and emotionally. I am my own worst enemy when it comes to completing the task in front of me. I put others' problems and helping them before myself, while I was breaking down, left with no energy. I would do something positive and read my Bible verses and pray. I felt unhappy most of the time dealing with grief and pain. I often read a poem to lift my spirits and turned on gospel music to get my worship and praise on.

In happy moments, I will always praise God, in difficult moments I will seek God. In the painful moments, I will forever trust God. I will always enjoy every moment to thank God for His plans for my life. The purpose of life is to enjoy every moment. I started volunteering for several ministries at church: The Pastoral Ministry, and the Benevolence Ministry were two, and I attended Cross College in 2011 at Family Christian Center.

In 2012 I attended a one-day Saturday New Membership class with my children. Two of their friends joined us at Family Christian Center. This was a great experience and God's hand was all over it. I have covenant with my children at a great church. I was faithful in paying my tithes, and I supported the vision of the church's ministries.

I started having problems with the spinal cord stimulator in my back in 2012. My knees were giving me a great deal of pain and once again limited my walking stability. I returned to the neurosurgeon and explained. I also needed to have an MRI on my knees. I could not have the test because of the spinal cord stimulator's not working properly. The neurosurgeon suggested the removal of the spinal cord stimulator, and since I was having more problems with the knees, it was best. I agreed, and the procedure took place in April of 2013. This was the fourth surgery and the last on my back. I fought hard to be strengthened and the spinal manipulation of the spinal cord stimulator did achieve the goal to help me walk, but now other health issues were present in my body.

I became more determined that I would fight the good fight of faith and be healed. I started focusing on what is in front of me: a vision of women in a support group to help one another through our physical health difficulties that brought us together.

The emotional stress of dealing with medications and loss of loved ones and chronic pain was effectively working against me. Once a week I attended a support group that was run by a psychologist. The group of ladies had a lot of breakthroughs, and I was getting my breakthrough by being obedient to God. I would pray before we dismissed the group and encourage all to come back the next week. There is supernatural power to be healthy and training our minds to be wealthy in physical and spiritual.

My prayer, "My Heavenly Father, I thank you that no weapon formed against me shall prosper and that every tongue and every word that rises against me in judgment the Lord will condemn. Thank you for covering me under your protection for my healing and restoration."

2 Timothy 4: 7-8

I have fought a good fight, I have finished my course, I have kept the faith: Henceforth there is laid up for me a crown of righteousness, which the Lord, the righteous judge, shall give me at that day: and not to me only, but unto all them also that love his appearing.

10

BREAKING THROUGH

And let us not be weary in well doing for in due season we
shall reap, if we faint not. ~ Galatians 6:9

I will always thank God for His goodness and righteousness. I will worship and praise Him through my life-difficulties and watch God restore me better than before. *Now faith is the substance of things hoped for, the evidence of things not seen.* ~Hebrews 11:1

I was at the breaking point in my life and prayed for new direction and wisdom from God. "Please, Lord, order my steps as you directed your son Jesus Christ." I understand more now that when Jesus is in control, failing is impossible.

When I was a young girl going to church, having my grandmother and aunts and uncles in the ministries as preachers, deacons, church mothers, and missionaries, I was covered under the blood of Jesus from the time I enter my mother's womb. I am who God says I am—a member of the royal priesthood in the Kingdom of God. The Lord is determined to build His church and it will be built first in me and you and the rest of our generations to come. It will always take obedience and sacrifices to finish this race on earth.

It takes strength to stand against the adversaries when you are going through life struggles. My physical injuries, health issues, and spirituality make me feel out of place. What a wakeup call to know you need to hold onto God's unchanging hands! When you are tired of running from God instead of running to Him and giving Him your problems, how in the world is He going to solve it when you are being disobedient? I have repented for not following His direction and I know the truth. Then you will know the truth, and the truth will make you free every time. (See John 8:32.)

The time is at hand to follow direction to enter the Kingdom of Holiness. I have read my Bible from beginning to end starting at the age of 10. The book of Jonah contains the story of Jonah who was in the stomach of a big whale. I am using Jonah here because I had a moment that I can relate to his character in the Bible. The challenge is my—and Jonah's—spirit of rebellion against God and failing to follow His directions. Jonah's disobedience caused him to get swallowed up by a big whale before he learned to listen to God. I had to pray like Jonah to the Lord my God to take me out of the deep waters and place my feet back on solid ground.

The pain and the disappointment when I ran from church to church looking for answers of salvation when I was young and healthy and had plenty of finances to back it up. The position I landed myself in with God was I did not want to follow the step-in ministries. I wanted to just be a bench member and stay safe and quiet and not be judged for sin in my life.

I had to fight through tough times and feeling the hurt, habits, and hang ups, repeatedly remembering feeling isolated because of my physical chronic pain and disability. The Lord's expectations of me were greater than my expectations of myself. I was swallowed up in this world system of judgment and attitudes towards me. I had to endure and wait for my change to come.

I was chosen by the director of the Psychiatric Department to be involved in the Peer Wellness Coach program in 2014 at John Stroger hospital for a six-week training program. This program's purpose is to mentor women on a voluntary assignment, working with doctors and substance abuse counselors. I finished the program and graduated in April 2014 with certification in Mental Health and Substance Abuse. The same year I was studying and in training for Eldership at Family Christian Center church. I attended Equip classes and training and graduated in June 2014 with a certificate of appointment for Eldership in the Ministries supported by our Pastor and overseen by lay members. My commission is to stand in the gap that often exists between the Pastor's vision and that of the congregation.

The strength to move forward and not look back to the past and focus on my future was difficult but essential. I did not focus on my physical condition or look the part of a handicapped individual. I just wanted to serve the Lord with all my heart and all my soul and allow myself to be led by the Spirit of God every day for the rest of my life. This was not so easy to do every day; there were challenging situations and relationship issues that kept me repenting constantly. You know that when you are being set up for a comeback the enemy will be trying to take you out. The important thing is to stand even if you are standing alone. If your heart is right and your actions follow your heart, you can be sure you know God has your back. The work as a minister in Eldership is not simply anointing people on the forehead with oil, but getting involved with praying over the members for health issues and comforting them through their life struggles, mostly hugging and, in the spirit of Christ, loving on them when there is a need to reach them.

My breakthrough happened when I stopped running away from the Lord Jesus Christ and ran to Him with open arms and let Him carry me from strength to strength and grace to grace with new mercy every day.

Jonah 2:9

But I will sacrifice unto thee with the voice of thanksgiving; I will pay that that I have vowed. Salvation is of the LORD.

11

BEST AND BETTER

Who his own self bares our sins in his own body on the tree, that we, being dead to sins, should live unto righteousness: by whose stripes ye were healed? ~ 1 Peter 2:24

In the beginning year of 2016, I was hospitalized due to chest pain and a lot of stressful situations in my life. I was in the hospital for three days and my family and church family were there to support and pray for me. I was visited by Pastor Utley early Sunday morning before church, and he anointed my head with oil and prayed for me. I know the Lord used him to encourage me to get up and proclaim my healing. I had tested the next day and all test results were negative, praise God for a good report! I was visited by Elder Dorothy, who is a prayer warrior, and she brought me communion and prayed. My blood pressure went down, and my chest pain went away. I was released that day. The power of prayers with two agreeing in spirit and in word proved that God was during it all.

There has been extreme pressure in my life. Dealing with my parents' death and with my physical conditions were stressful time for me. I had decided to invest my time in prevention, intervention, and recovery of my own health. I wanted the best that life had to offer, along with better ways of handling my medical complications. It

PHYSICALLY **STRENGTHENED** SPIRITUALLY **DRIVEN**

takes real strength to stand on God's promises of goodness and mercy every day and every way. My dear friends, please never, never give up. Don't give up on God because He certainly won't give up on you.

The faith to pray continued for diabetes, high blood pressure, my physical body, depression, and anxiety with being severely overweight was enough. All this did was bring me closer to the Lord for His grace is sufficient. I had to learn patience and not to fear the storms in my life that were out of control. I worked on encouraging myself, and I was steadfast to pursue, overtake, and recover all that the enemy had taken from me. "The Lord, strong and mighty, will heal me" was my frame of mind. I had to stay strong in my faith and I will always live happy if I live with a positive mind and heart. I empty myself before the power and strength of the Lord Jesus Christ. I will let God's spiritual guidance fill me up.

What kept me balanced and working on my chronic physical condition was prayer and faith along with the help of my family and church family. This journey had been long and now was the time to trust like never. I need to stay quiet and humbled because the promises of the Lord are yes and amen. I called on the name of Jehovah Jireh who is my provider and my healer. I cannot heal myself and the doctors cannot heal me in the aspects of stopping the pain completely. I have learned it is better to accept the health issues and deal with them as I walk with the Lord. I learned my strengths are best activated by dealing through time and faith to achieve restoration in my body.

The training and experience as a Wellness Coach working as a volunteer at John Stronger Hospital has been valuable to me. I attended a conference to promote wellness in the eight dimensions of recovery:

- Physical
- Social
- Spiritual
- Occupational
- Emotional
- Environmental
- Financial
- Intellectual

This is how I learned to maintain a healthy balance in my life. It helps with stressful situations and keeps me alert when I anticipate a crisis is about to happen. The Vision of Wellness is a support group supporting women recovering from mental health issues and substance abuse; it encourages them to incorporate wellness in order to improve their overall quality of life. There are no excuses if you use the tools to get well and faith to succeed in reaching your goals.

The better and best example comes with exercises in my body, mind, and soul. This requires listening to the advice of your doctor(s) and family. When your doctor(s) see your potential and strengths they more likely will have your best interest when you are honest and express your desire to live your life without strong pain medications that would be addictive. We need physicians in our lives for regular checkups and blood pressure checks and other disorders. In the Bible, Luke was a great Physician and Paul apparently saw physicians because he had what he called a thorn in his flesh. The doctor(s) can help prolong your life with the help of the Lord and faith.

I stayed on top of my health issue and reported when something was feeling wrong. The confidence of knowing that there are doctor(s) who take time to assure that you are moving in the right direction concerning your health is invaluable. I need to be very consistent in getting the proper sleep and meditating on the Word of God.

I often go beyond my physical abilities helping others and volunteering in many organizations. The positive words of affirmation, "I will live with the right consciousness and not through negative emotion" have made a difference in my thinking. I made a decree that every day for the rest of my life I will do my best. I want to enjoy the peace, joy, and happiness that comes from knowing that my best days are in front of me.

I started physical therapy for my knees and lower back to relieve the pain and to strengthen my physical body because I was dealing with weaknesses, numbness, and pain in my joints. This assessment and evaluation were so different from the previous physical therapist. I learned more about the conditions of my physical injuries and the importance of stretching, along with training the body to heal safely without further injuries.

The physical therapist Tom from Community Hospital Fitness Pointe worked with me for several weeks. He showed me the mechanics of the body along with the back and knee systems' functionality that must be protected to stay strong. He stressed to me that the way we walk and carry ourselves on our weight-bearing joints is important; he told me the changes we must make in correcting the posture to decrease the knee and back pain, having consistency going swimming and using weight-bearing machines to strengthen our joints.

The benefits of exercise can increase the amount of muscle in our body and give us energy and curb our appetite and decrease stress. I had to get the weight off to be productive in my recovery for my knees and back. I was trying to prevent having a total knee replacement currently. I thank God for sending people into my life to help me by training me to be better in my physical as well as my spiritual life journey. The Word of God says in Joel 3:10b, . . .*let the weak say, I am strong*. I am strong enough to make it. I am keeping the faith.

The miracle month at Family Christian Church in April 2016, with our guest Pastor Tim Storey on a Wednesday night was a fantastic night. I had hidden my physical challenge which was revealed to all at the church;

he prophesied about my life and my healing. I have lived with my hidden disability for so long and people sometimes wondered what is wrong, but I am happy it is out now. This was real and I had the faith to agree by praising and singing and dancing before the church. "I AM HEALED!"

The best way to socialize with people is to have compassion, kindness, and grace. I attended Cross College Ministry courses on January 24, 2011, with Pastor Steve Munsey teaching Journey *through the Bible* from Genesis to the book of Revelation. The ten-week curriculum was worth pursuing. I began to meet other instructors and Pastor Ponder and Pastor Utley and their ministry classes. The classroom activities and participation were absolutely wonderful. I received my Diploma and graduated in June of 2016 to further strengthen my capacity to minister in the Church.

I began to meet great people. My classmates had a gathering after graduation. I adored and adopted Mrs. Giragos and Renée Giragos as my spiritual mother and sister; I called her "Momma G." We graduated from Cross College together and have studies and long talks both in person and on the phone. I trust and respect them so much and I am so happy and encouraged to have them a part of my life and journey. Our relationship keeps growing and Momma G has taught me spiritual etiquette. First, she welcomed me into her family and introduced me to the

Women's Association of the Northwest Indiana Symphony Society in July 2016, where I became a member and met amazing women in this organization.

The positive changes in my life resulting from going to church have increased my faith and decreased my stress in dealing with chronic pain and health challenges. The Lord has directed my heart into God's love and Christ's preservation of who I am.

I am a survivor and I am strong, and I AM a woman after God's own heart. My problems strengthen me and solving problems has impacted me. I will ride over the storms; I cannot be distracted while continuously waiting for my miracles. I can't let anyone hurt my feelings and destroy my God-given destiny. I am trusting and believing for my breakthrough and NO obstacle can stop it and NO limitation can prevent it and NO enemy can stand against it. I will have a prosperous conclusion of my health and wealth, and I will pay a vow that I made to the Lord in secret. The Word says I can ask anything in His name, and He will do it. Having courage does not mean that we are unafraid. Having courage and showing courage means we face our fears. We can say, " I have fallen but I will get up."

Ephesians 6:10-20

10 Finally, my brethren, be strong in the Lord, and in the power of his might.

11 Put on the whole armor of God, that ye may be able to stand against the wiles of the devil.

12 For we wrestle not against flesh and blood, but against principalities, against powers, against the rulers of the darkness of this world, against spiritual wickedness in high *places*.

13 Wherefore take unto you the whole armor of God, that ye may be able to withstand in the evil day, and having done all, to stand.

14 Stand therefore, having your loins girt about with truth, and having on the breastplate of righteousness.

15 And your feet shod with the preparation of the gospel of peace.

16 Above all, taking the shield of faith, wherewith ye shall be able to quench all the fiery darts of the wicked.

17 And take the helmet of salvation, and the sword of the Spirit, which is the word of God:

18 Praying always with all prayer and supplication in the Spirit and watching thereunto with all perseverance and supplication for all saints.

19 And for me, that utterance may be given unto me, that I may open my mouth boldly, to make known the mystery of the gospel,

20 For which I am an ambassador in bonds: that therein I may speak boldly, as I ought to speak.

12

CELEBRATING LIFE AGAIN

*Jesus saith unto him, I am the way, the truth, and the life:
no man cometh unto the Father, but by me. ~ John 14:6*

I've traveled back down memory lane to write this book. I begin today a new life, starting over in a new direction. I have had to keep up with my physical strength and working on my inner and outer appearance daily. The issues of the chronic pain remain inside of me and what those inner issues look like on the outside of me could be a challenge. I have had to lose weight to relieve the discomforts of pain off my knees to be able to walk. The healing power of prayers drive me closer to God daily.

I have been to many physicians for help with back and knee treatments and have taken many medications to relieve pain and other medical conditions. I had been on so many medications. I was taking strong opioids pills that could make you wonder how I was able to function. The long-term use of any medication to relieve a medical condition has side effects and can lead to dependency. The prescriptions for strong pain medication are powerful drugs that interfere with the nervous system's transmission of the nerve signals we perceive as pain. The problem with this is that pain medicines simply mask the pain for which they are taken. They do not cure. Taking opioids long-term causes more health problems, and a serious risk of respiratory system failures or death.

I need to manage my pain before it manages me. I am thankful that I have a say in my treatment regarding avoiding being on strong pain medications. I thank God I was allergic to medicines that were addictive. I again was told that both of my knees were bone on bone and that I would need a knee replacement surgery in 2016. The medical evidence proved it was true. I wasn't ready to go that way because of my other medical conditions. I was fearful. My father had the surgery for his knees and eventually he failed to survive due to complications from his diabetes. I prayed and sought God for another way other than another surgery. I was at the point of declaring NO MORE surgery after four back surgeries and a foot surgery. I had just had enough of surgeries.

For God hath not given us the spirit of fear; but of power, and of love, and of a sound mind. ~ 2 Timothy 1:7

I had to be still and know that God is in control and simply wait on God. In beginning of 2017, I researched other ways of relieving my knee pain by going to a free screening at the Joint Relief Institute for Non-Surgical Joint Arthritis treatment. The Physician took X-rays and explained, showing me what is going on with my knees, and I my confidence to start the treatment with Dr. Hana was renewed. I was able to see through the motion-imaging camera the medicine going into the right place in my knees. Only days after the treatment I noticed that there was a decrease in pain, and swelling was going down with no cracking and popping in my knees. I had four weekly injections of treatment in each knee. I was able to resume my exercise at the fitness center and begin to lose weight. Working with a nutritionist, a health coach, and family members on dieting and weight loss drinks. I was getting positive results by not being afraid and getting on with planning my future. I was so thankful for the Joint Relief Institute and the doctor(s) and staff for making me feel alive and my knees pain-free. I was able to return to working out in the gym with a trainer and swimming exercises.

For she said within herself, If I may but touch his garment, I shall be whole. ~ Matthew 9:21

The example of the many people who were healed because of their faith was evident in the Bible and not a fairytale story. It was the real-life testimony and was recorded for such a time in my life to help me hold onto my faith and be real. Re-reading the story of the woman with the issue of blood made me desire so desperately to have a touch of the almighty God and His Son Jesus who restored health in her body after twelve years. She spent money and time going to physicians until she had no more money and probably little time. One day she encountered The Great Physician, Jesus Christ, and she believed if she could only touch His garment she would be restored to health. The Lord Jesus realized that someone touched

Him, turned around and saw her and said to her, "Take courage, daughter, your faith has made you whole."

The woman was restored to health immediately. I can relate to this woman; and I can tell you that for twenty plus years I have been going through life coping with my physical conditions, seeing many health professionals hoping to be well in all areas of my health. I had diabetes that has affected my eyes and kidneys with high blood pressure, and this runs strong in my family members.

I prayed, "Jesus please continue to help me keep my faith strong and never let go but hold on to You." In a world full of "no," God says "yes," and it is possible; and what you ask, you shall receive. It's so important for my future that I grow in faith, which shows confidence and trust in God. I had to conquer my fears and press to the other side. I needed to accept peace and happiness amid the storm and not give into the emotional wreck that the devil would have me bound in all the time.

I began to connect with others and develop a support system, expanding my sense of purpose and meaning in life. I expressed my feelings and love to people I trusted. I was managing effectively with life's challenges. I started appreciating nature and the beauty that surrounded me. I started making social connections by going to fundraisers to support the Women's Association of the Northwest Indiana Symphony Society in May 2017, enjoying the festivities. I was in a hat contest and won for Design. This was my first time appearing in the <u>Times</u> newspaper or any newspaper. I started feeling good about my resolution to be strengthened and appreciated in my life journey.

The month before the fundraiser I was nominated by Vice-President of Membership, Mrs. Giragos, for the Women's Association of the Northwest Indiana Symphony Society Board of Directors. I was chosen in July of 2017, and I accepted the invitation to join the Board of Directors. I like supporting a cause that helps young people and especially music that relaxes and calms your spirit. This position took me back to when I was teenaged, playing the drums. As an adult, I love different genres of music. I thank my sponsors for accepting me to be on the Board of Director; it has brightened my horizons.

I am God's workmanship created to do great things for him. ~ Ephesians 2:10

Victorious strength comes from God's sending me into new areas and changing my direction. I discovered values and principles and beliefs that are important for growth. You don't have to live below your privileges because of your past experiences and your current situations. I am a child of the Almighty God, and He desires me to be happy and to be in good health as my soul prospers. (See 3 John, verse 2.) He will send important people into your life to help you rise and not push you down. It is important to hang on to positive people going somewhere and not leading you to nowhere. The deep calls for the deep, and I want to go deep into God's plans for my life. I had to learn who Lisa Tyree is and what her purpose for life on earth needs to be. First, I wanted to know where the name came from and if it is a Biblical name. The name <u>Lisa</u> is a Hebrew name and comes from Elizabeth and Elisheba, meaning either oath of God, or God's satisfaction and devoted to God. I needed to go deeper into my destiny.

I knew that I needed to go on a spiritual journey, one that would speak to my spirit, giving me an answer to my future. My church, Family Christian Center, under the supervision of Senior Pastors Steve and Melodye Munsey, planned a trip "THE BEST OF ISRAEL." Israel, the country, is often referred to as the Holy Land. A journey included following in the footsteps of Jesus, and I wanted to go. It was made possible. I was able to pay for the all-inclusive journey which included everything needed. I just needed to pack and go for the journey of a lifetime. The Holy Land experience to ISRAEL in November 2017 proved to be all that I had read about as a young girl, and I viewed it with my own eyes in the beautiful nine days touring.

We had seventy people from the church traveling with our Pastors and the journey began as we departed from Chicago O'Hare International and arrived in Frankfurt, Germany and then on to Tel-Aviv, ISRAEL where there was an eight-hour difference in time. We had to adjust after the long flight and the change in time.

We had the best representation from Noseworthy Travel Service meeting us at the airport with two nice Deluxe Motor coaches. We went to the first hotel in Tiberius for three days' overnight stay. We had dinner and the food was fresh and good. We walked around the hotel and went to bed early, rising in the morning in good time for our journey and sightseeing. First, Caesarea on the Mediterranean Sea, and Mt. Carmel, Megiddo the Valley of Armageddon. We saw the city of Nazareth, the boyhood home of Jesus. As we drove by Cana, the location of his first miracle, the transformation of water into wine at the marriage of Cana, we were delighted to look at the high mountains. We went back to Tiberius, to our hotel for dinner and to rest for the next day's touring.

We had young teenagers as well as Mother Smith, the oldest member, traveling with us. I **had** to keep up with Mother Smith; she is twice my age and was concerned about the physical condition of my knees. I had to stop and rest, slowing down at times. I was not about to let the condition of my arthritic knees hinder me from continuing to walk in faith for my healing and deliverance.

The beautiful boat rides on the Sea of Galilee, the Biblical stories by our pastor, and the praise and worship of our groups traveling together in the footstep of Jesus and his disciples were magnificent. I gained Biblical and spiritual revelations plus a lot of knowledge of history. There was a lot of revealing of the future and I wished I had my family on this journey with me. We were baptized by our Pastor Munsey in the Jordan River baptismal site; what a multitude of people were getting baptized! It felt so good to renew my life and the anointing in my body. This was worth the journey. We returned to our hotel for dinner and to rest and pack for the next day when we would be traveling to Jerusalem.

That he would grant you, according to the riches of his glory, to be strengthened with might by his Spirit in the inner man;
~Ephesians 3:16

My roommate and traveling companion were my godmother's sister, Tami, and we had so much fun and many girl-time discussions in our room. She was such an amazing and peaceful roommate and there were no issues. We watched over one another and took plenty of pictures to send back home. We brought back rocks and holy water We left Galilee to travel by coach bus to Jerusalem, staying at the Crown Plaza Hotel and touring the rest of the Holy Land.

We traveled to see the Mount of Olives to view the "Golden City." There we all took a group picture. Many of the travelers with us were thrilled at seeing the camels and donkey; it wasn't as fascinating to me because well, I see that at church during *Jesus of Nazareth* story. (If you're reading my book please come during March and April; you get to see the real deal.) I saw the Garden of Gethsemane where Jesus prayed before He was betrayed.

I had to forgive people secretly who have betrayed my trust, but it is not for them to know, but for me to be free. I thank the Lord for this: He loved Judas even when He knew he disliked and falsely accused Him. The Lord Jesus was innocent, but He did his Father's will. Can you pray for one hour for yourself and others? The best way to find yourself is to lose yourself in the service of the almighty God.

We were again on our way and our stop on that day was at the Western Wall, called the Wailing Wall. We stopped there for prayer and our church mission. Many people at FCC had written prayer requests, and our mission was to deliver the prayer cards and pray for the peace of Jerusalem. What a beautiful place to visit!

I brought with me prayer requests from friends and people in my doctors' offices who knew I was going and asked if I would take their prayer requests. I did and this further met my expectations by praying at the Wailing Wall and stuffing prayer requests into the wall. Our Pastor Steve spoke a word and we prayed for our church members' prayer requests, releasing the blessing on the thousands of prayer cards sent with us to be prayed over and placed into the Wailing Wall.

The next site to visit was Mount Zion where we viewed the Upper Room where the Holy Ghost fell on the people gathered there on the Day of Pentecost, a Jewish Feast Day. One hundred and twenty were filled. This was amazing to see! I walked through the house of Caiaphas, the High Priest, where they held Jesus before His crucifixion.

This was a spiritual awaking for me. I experienced a drive to learn more of Jesus' suffering in His physical body, realizing my situation is no comparison. I am humbled to stand and keep moving and never look back in my past again to ask why this physical condition is with me.

The journey to see the town of Bethlehem where Jesus was born was important to me. There we viewed the Church of the Nativity, and we met with the Governor inside the Church of Nativity. The amount of gold and the images on the walls were amazing. Our church family took a group picture in front of this beautiful church attraction that many people—not only Christians—come to visit. We headed back to the bus where we were taken to see the Shepherds' Fields and we managed to get in some shopping before returning to our hotel for dinner, fellowship, and rest.

The next morning, we went to visit Masada National Park where our church group traveled across in the cable cars overlooking over the mountains; however, some of our group bravely walked up the steep mountain. The cable cars provided the only access for people who have disabilities to get to the top. When traveling in the air on cable cars, you sit still and trust God to get you there. Looking over the mountains below us was amazing and walking the grounds of ancient history was fascinating.

The next place I enjoyed visiting was the Dead Sea. The buoyancy and medicinal benefits are world-renowned for healing by saltwater mixed with the muddy water. I walked to the water with Mother Smith, who was ninety; we sat in the chairs and I washed her feet in the saltwater. I prayed and looked up at the sky and felt the presence of the Lord healing all who believe. I felt great in my body and thanked God for allowing me to be here in ISRAEL. The tourist guide's famous words were, "Come, come and see the beautiful place."

Our next day's journey was to the Holocaust History Museum, the memorial to the six million Jews—some of whom were small children—by German Nazi soldiers in the time leading up to World War II. This was not so exciting to see, knowing what had happened during the dictatorial regime of Adolf Hitler. The tour of what happened in the gas chambers and the display of innocent lives gone as many fled for safety was heart-rending. I learned some history of the fighting between the Germans and Jews. You must be spiritually driven to understand the fear of losing your life over someone else controlling your destiny. (See my explanation of my statement regarding what happened to me in Frankfort, Germany coming back to the United States later in this chapter.)

The next piece of our tour was to the Pool of Bethesda, the place where Jesus healed on the Sabbath. I had been waiting to be healed of my physical condition and having faith and hope for my new beginning as I am made whole to rise and walk. We visited the Garden Tomb which is found outside Jerusalem's city walls. We walked through and investigated where the burial and resurrection of Jesus Christ, and near was Gordon's Calvary. We all sat down, and Pastor Steve taught us the Biblical truths of Jesus' burial. He also served us communion as we praised and worshiped the risen Lord Jesus Christ Who is sitting on the right hand of God. The ISRAEL tour would not have been complete without seeing this special place and feeling the presence of our Lord and Savior Jesus Christ. Yes, He has risen.

This was the end of our journey. It was time to go back to the hotel and pack to get ready to return to the United States. We were heading home with a great impression of the Holy Land. We had an early morning flight leaving on Tuesday from Tel-Aviv, ISRAEL, going to Frankfurt, GERMANY, and everything went okay, the checked bags and carry-on bag having been sent through a scanner and onto plane.

Our plane landed in Frankfurt, GERMANY, and our group was separated. My carryon bag went through scanner, and I was pulled aside from the rest of the group. Obviously, I had something in my carryon bag that alarmed the officer and the police came to take me to another area in the airport that separated me from the church travelers. I was told I had a bullet in my purse, and they asked where I just flew from. I told them ISRAEL and that's when they showed me my purse inside the carry-on and asked if it belonged to me. I stated yes, it is my purse, but I did not know I had a bullet in my purse. I was held for ninety minutes. Because I told the truth and they had my passport and ran a background check on me, I was found to have credentials for security back in the United States and that I was not a threat. I did not have a gun and the mistake was only one cartilage that they kept in their possession. I was never fingerprinted, or photos taken; neither did I leave out of the airport. I was treated with respect and handled very carefully. I prayed for the Almighty Lord to help me get out of this mess. They finally let me go but the plane with my church family had already taken off and they had no idea that I was not on the plane. I had to purchase another plane ticket and had fifteen minutes to get to the other side of the airport or I would be staying overnight in Frankfort, Germany. After having seen in the Museum the story of the Jews killed, I wanted badly to go home. I hurried to the other side, taking a train through the airport to the international connections gates and had to walk the rest of the way to the gate.

The walking—especially trying to hurry—exhausted me. He came through just when I said, "Please Lord, help me." A cart full of people stopped and made room for me to get on, and it took me to my gate. I had just made it to the gate when I saw steward about to close the door. I said, "Wait, please." I had made it by the grace of God! I am thankful for Jesus who carried me through to get home safely. This was an eight-hour trip in the air going to New Jersey (New York transfer), and I felt alone but Jesus was there all the time.

But go rather to the lost sheep of the house of Israel.
~Matthew 10:6

I was the lost sheep of our group and there was no fear because when the Pastors realized I was not with them, they called the church to contact Pastor John Ponder and my family and let them know that I had missed my plane. They all were praying and concerned about what might happen to me. I am part of a praying church, and I am a praying woman. This was my time for the Lord Jesus to reveal to me my true calling and knowing that He had always been with me. I just received the confirmation directly from my experiences.

I was not angered or upset with my church family at all. This was my time with Jesus to reflect on what it means to be faithful, being really tested, experiencing trials. I had to wait on another flight to return to O'Hare Airport, but I

had favor in the air praying for the sick and telling my story and the praise report that Jesus is the true Messiah and I am His child. I returned home just a couple of hours after the other group. When I returned home, my family was more loving, and I was truly missed.

I was totally sold out for the Lord Jesus Christ and praying and being happy that I had experienced so much on that journey. It is difficult for people to understand that I draw my strength from troubles; I will smile during distress and I will grow stronger with prayer and hope for the future. I am covered by the blood of Jesus Christ. I am spiritually driven due to my experience in ISRAEL and will continue to be physically strengthened.

I am celebrating now in January of 2018; I was healed of diabetes and I was taken off the medication. My hypertension was under control and high cholesterol was well under control. I am taking less pain medication, and I am not walking with the help of any devices. The Lord has performed my healing process and miracles are still working in my life. The Lord's healing power was on the backside of Calvary and the blood that cleanses us every day was the front side of Calvary. I am still working in faith for all my pain in my joints to be healed with deliverance every day, and I know someday my change will finally come.

1 Peter 3:12

For the eyes of the Lord are over the righteous, and his ears are open unto their prayers: but the face of the Lord is against them that do evil.

1 Peter 3:13

And who is he that will harm you, if ye be followers of that which is good?

1 Peter 3:14

But and if ye suffer for righteousness' sake, happy are ye: and be not afraid of their terror, neither be troubled.

PICTURES OF THE ISRAEL EXPERIENCE

The following pages are just a few pictures from author's life-changing trip to Israel with her home church, Family Christian Center. She, along with several other church members, were joined by their senior pastors, Dr. Steve and Melodye Munsey to experience the journey of a lifetime.

At the Garden Tomb
Where Jesus' body was placed!

Lisa R. Tyree

*On the first day of the week, very early in the morning, the women took the spices they had prepared and went to the **tomb**. They found the stone rolled away from the **tomb**, but when they entered, they did not find the body of the Lord Jesus.*

Luke 24:1-3

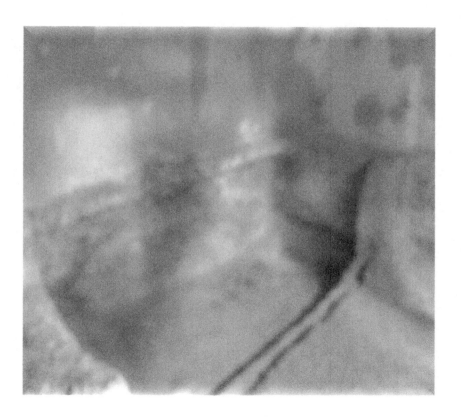

Lisa R. Tyree

At the Wailing Wall

Author, Lisa Tyree, is praying for healing over the prayer request cards given to her from other patients from her doctor's office.

Lisa R. Tyree